TORNADO TERROR

ALSO BY LAUREN TARSHIS

I SURVIVED

TRUE STORIES

TORNADO TERROR

Lauren Tarshis

SCHOLASTIC PRESS / NEW YORK

Library of Congress Cataloging-in-Publication Data available

ISBN 978-0-545-91943-2

10 9 8 7 6 5 4 3 2 1   17 18 19 20 21

Printed in the U.S.A.   23

First edition, March 2017

Book design by Deborah Dinger

For Deb Dinger Butler

IN THIS BOOK

77 THE EVIL SWIRLING DARKNESS
THE JOPLIN TORNADO OF 2011

This is one of the first
photos of a tornado,
taken in 1884, in Kansas.
People were so fascinated
by this picture that it
was sold as a postcard.

THE DEVIL'S WIND

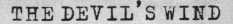

Imagine it's two hundred years ago. You're walking alone somewhere in the middle of America. There are no towns, no roads, and not another person around for miles. Suddenly the sky turns greenish black. The wind starts to howl. And then you see it, a strange swirling cloud snaking down from the sky. It roars to life, and starts tearing across the land, shattering everything in its path.

Your heart stops. Your blood runs cold. What could this be?

Today, of course, you would know that it's a tornado.

But until about the middle of the 1800s, few people in the world had heard of these monstrous clouds. For centuries, the only people who had witnessed them were people living on America's plains—members of Native American nations. Members of the Miami tribe called them the devil's wind. The Kiowa told of a beast called the Storm-Maker Red Horse, a flying horse with a snakelike tail that whipped through the sky to create tornadoes.

This is a piece of a calendar drawn by a Kiowa artist, in 1905. The image on the far right shows the Storm-Maker Red Horse, which many Kiowa believed caused tornadoes.

When early American settlers first witnessed tornadoes, they had no idea what they were. Some thought they were curses, or warnings from the heavens.

It wasn't until the 1870s that scientists started to really study them, and that they agreed on the name tornado.

Since that time, thousands of tornadoes have struck the United States, smashing cities, wiping away towns, and destroying lives. On the following pages, you will read about two famously terrible tornadoes—the Tri-State Tornado of 1925 and the Joplin Tornado of 2011. I chose to write about these two because they were especially powerful and destructive. And together, they show how our understanding of tornadoes has changed over the decades.

What hasn't changed is their shocking power. These devilish winds are every bit as terrifying and fascinating as they were centuries ago.

"EVERYBODY MUST BE DEAD"

THE TRI-STATE TORNADO, 1925

Eleven-year-old Adrian Dillon had heard stories about ferocious monsters lurking near his Illinois town. There was the Ozark Howler, a wild bearlike creature with razor-sharp teeth and a bellowing roar. There was the Murphysboro Mud Monster, a seven-foot giant with two-inch teeth.

But Adrian was about to come face-to-face with a real monster, one far more ferocious than any from a legend or ghost story.

It was the Tri-State Tornado, the deadliest single tornado ever to strike the United States. It roared out of the sky on March 18, 1925. In roughly three hours, the massive twister ripped through Missouri, Illinois, and Indiana. It killed nearly seven hundred people. It destroyed twelve schools. Entire towns were sucked into the sky.

One of those towns was Parrish, Illinois, where Adrian lived with his family.

There are many legends
about fearsome creatures
lurking in the wilderness
of Southern Illinois.

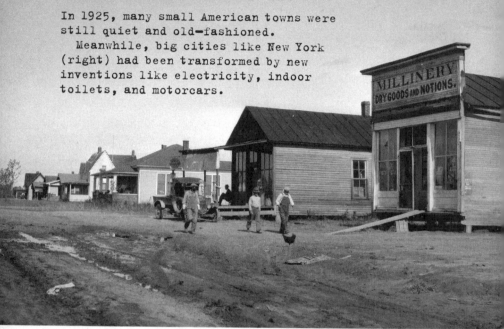

SMALL TOWNS VS. BIG CITIES

In 1925, many small American towns were still quiet and old-fashioned.

Meanwhile, big cities like New York (right) had been transformed by new inventions like electricity, indoor toilets, and motorcars.

AN EXCITING DAY AHEAD

Adrian woke up on the morning of March 18 with a jolt of excitement. Not much ever happened in Parrish. It was just a tiny speck of a town, nestled within the grassy hills of Southern Illinois.

America was changing fast in 1925, with most cities and big towns lit up by electric lights and honking with motorcars.

But Parrish hadn't changed much since Adrian's grandparents first settled here one hundred years before. Parrish School didn't have electricity yet. Few people had telephones or radios. Many people in Parrish, including the Dillons, still drove around in wagons pulled by horses.

But for Adrian, Parrish was the center of the world. Especially today. Because this afternoon

In the 1920s, marbles was the most popular game for American boys.

In many cities, marbles tournaments attracted huge crowds.

Marbles could be played anywhere— even behind a school's toilet! In the 1920s, many schools still had only outdoor toilets.

TOILET

While marbles was played mainly by boys, the game of jacks was a favorite for girls.

was the town's big marbles tournament. Adrian had permission to leave school early to compete.

Marbles was one of the most popular games in America in 1925, and Adrian and his friends were fanatics. They played every day at recess. Adrian and his friends would kneel around a big circle they'd drawn in the ground. They would take turns trying to knock one another's marbles out of the dirt ring. Adrian loved everything about the game—the feel of cool glass marble in his hand, the clack of the marbles, the hoots and shouts of his buddies.

And, of course, Adrian loved to win. He would never brag, but he was one of the best shooters at Parrish School.

True, there were only about eighty kids. But still. Adrian was proud of his skill. His prized possession was a sack filled with marbles he'd won in matches. If he did well in today's tournament, he'd be the town's marbles champion. His photo would be in the newspaper. He'd be famous!

Adrian lay under his quilt, smiling to himself.

But suddenly the sound of his father's voice snapped him out of his happy spell. Even a marble champion had to do his morning chores.

A HAPPY FAMILY

Adrian hopped out of bed and quickly threw on the worn trousers and shirt he wore every day to school. The sun was barely up, but already the Dillon household was buzzing with action.

The family lived on one of the small farms that surrounded Parrish. And there was always work to be done—horses and goats and cows to care for, buckets of water to fill from the well, fences to

SCENES OF 1920s FARM LIFE

There are no surviving photographs of the Dillons' farm. But these photos capture what life was like in farming areas like Parrish.

mend, fields to weed. That morning, Adrian and his thirteen-year-old brother, Leonard, milked the cows. Ten-year-old Ruie helped prepare the oatmeal and bacon for breakfast. Even little Wendell and Faye pitched in by feeding the family's pet rabbits.

The work was endless. But Adrian knew the family was lucky to have their farm. Many of

Adrian's friends' fathers worked in the dangerous
Black Star Coal Mine, one of the many mines dug
under the hills of southern Missouri and Illinois.
Being a miner meant working hundreds of feet
underground in almost total darkness. Miners
breathed in poisonous dust and faced the constant
risk of explosions and cave-ins. Hundreds of
miners died every year in America.

FAMILY FUN IN THE 1920s

In the evenings, many families gathered around their radios to listen to concerts and comedy shows.

Farming was a safer job than mining. And the Dillon house was a happy one.

Adrian's mom and dad—Edna and John—had a loving marriage. Edna doted on the kids and their animals. John was a warm man with many friends.

After chores, the family sat down together for breakfast. At 8:00 a.m., Adrian, Leonard, and Ruie left for school, about a mile walk. Adrian waved to his mom and brother and sister.

He would never see his house again.

THE RAGING STORM

The Dillon kids walked to school under a bright blue sky. The day was much warmer and more humid than usual. The blueberry bushes were in bloom, and wildflowers were starting to peek their bright heads up through the tall grass. The warm breeze made Ruie's braids dance around her shoulders. All seemed peaceful.

And yet hundreds of miles to the west, a monstrous storm was raging. Overnight, violent thunderstorms lashed Oklahoma and Kansas. Egg-size hailstones had shattered windows and punched holes in rooftops. A small tornado had chewed apart a barn in a small Kansas town.

That storm had crossed into Missouri from Kansas, and was heading east. It was gaining strength and moving at 70 miles per hour, faster than a train.

Those summery breezes following the Dillon kids to school would make the storm even more dangerous. Warm, moist air adds power to thunderstorms, and makes tornadoes more likely.

But nobody in and around Parrish knew that a ferocious storm had set its sights on their town. The weather forecast printed in most area newspapers that morning said simply that rain was possible for later in the afternoon.

In fact, most US weather reports were wrong in 1925. The science of weather, called meteorology, was still new. There were no high-tech tools for tracking storms as they moved across the country. Weather forecasts were more like guesses than scientific predictions.

Weather disasters often struck with no warning at all. Most famously, in 1900, a massive hurricane

The hurricane that hit Galveston, Texas, in 1900 killed eight thousand people. It is still the deadliest hurricane in US history.

The Galveston Daily News.

90TH YEAR—NO 173. GALVESTON, TEXAS, THURSDAY,- SEPTEMBER 13 1900 ESTABLISHED 1842

STORY OF THE GREAT DISASTER AT GALVESTON

Loss of Life Is Estimated at Between 4000 and 5000---Not a Single Individual Escaped Property Loss---The Total Property Loss From Fifteen to Twenty Million Dollars.

hit the city of Galveston, Texas. Days before, ship captains at sea had warned that a wild storm was heading north, toward America's southern coast. But meteorologists did not believe the storm would hit Galveston. They were wrong. It slammed into the city, flooding some neighborhoods under twenty feet of churning water. Approximately eight thousand people died.

NO TORNADO WARNINGS

By 1925, scientists still couldn't accurately predict the path of big storms. But that's not the only reason there were no tornado warnings on March 18. The very word—*tornado*—was actually banned from US government weather reports. Meteorologists weren't allowed to use the word in their forecasts. That had been the rule in the United States since the late 1880s. The word *tornado* was too frightening, some believed. People might panic if they thought a tornado could strike. And besides, tornadoes were almost impossible to predict. Why terrify people when most likely the warning would be wrong?

And so the thousands of people in the storm's path on March 18 went about their day. Men went to work in the mines. Adrian's dad was preparing to plant his fields. Most women stayed home to care for their little children. None had any hint that disaster was about to strike.

THE FIRST VICTIMS

Adrian, Leonard, and Ruie settled in at Parrish School, a brick building not far from the center of town. Like most country schools in the 1920s, Parrish School was a one-room schoolhouse. There was just one teacher in charge of about forty kids aged six to fourteen. Little kids practiced their letters, scratching away on small slate chalkboards they kept at their desks. Older kids worked on grammar and math and took turns reciting poems they'd memorized.

At recess, Adrian practiced his marbles shots.

It was just a typical day in Parrish. Nobody could imagine the disaster that was about to come.

ONE TEACHER FOR ALL
There are no surviving photographs of Adrian's school in Parrish, but this photo shows an American schoolhouse from the early 1900s.

The Tri-State Tornado was born at about 1:00 P.M., in a Missouri forest 150 miles west of Parrish. It was just a ropy little funnel when it dropped from the sky. But it was still powerful enough to chew apart trees and scatter their branches. Animals scurried into their burrows. Birds huddled in bushes. A farmer named Sam Flowers was riding his horse through the woods, with his loyal dog trotting behind.

INSTANT DEATH

Flowers must have heard the tornado's roar before he saw the swirling funnel. It grabbed him off his horse and threw him to the ground. Before

Flowers could get up, a tree fell on top of him. He was killed instantly.

His horse made it back home safely. Hours later, Flowers was discovered by his family. They were guided to his body by the dog's frantic barks. The loyal mutt had not left her master's side.

After killing Sam Flowers, the tornado sped northeast, still moving at more than 70 miles an hour. At about 1:15 P.M., it reached the small town of Annapolis, Missouri, home to about nine hundred people.

Whoosh!

In less than one minute, the tornado destroyed all but seven of the town's eighty-five homes. Annapolis School, a small stone building, was smashed into rubble with its thirty-two students inside. Main Street's shops and restaurants were swept away.

Incredibly, the tornado took the lives of only four people in Annapolis. All thirty-two of the schoolchildren climbed out of the rubble alive. So did almost everyone trapped inside ruined homes and shops. Most of the men in town were working in a nearby mine, which protected them from the tornado's fury. For once, working hundreds of feet underground was a blessing.

The tornado roared out of Annapolis and whirled across miles of thick forests and craggy hills until it reached the small town of Biehle.

Whoosh!

It devoured homes and farms and killed seventeen people before setting its sights on the town's school, Garver. As it passed over the school, it lifted the entire building off the ground. Inside were twenty-five kids and their young teacher, Miss Bengert. Like a giant bird gripping a terrified rabbit in its claws, the tornado carried the school for hundreds of yards. As the building broke apart in midair, the children and their teacher were scattered into fields surrounding Biehle.

Incredibly, the students and their teacher all survived.

A HUNGRY BEAST

By now the tornado had been on the ground for more than an hour, which was highly unusual. Most tornadoes are fragile creations. Of the more than 1,200 tornadoes that strike America every year, most are wispy funnels that fall lazily out of the sky, blow over a few trees and mailboxes, and then quickly fall apart. A typical tornado stays on the ground for about ten minutes before it loses strength.

What made the Tri-State Tornado so unique—and horrifying—was that it did not lose power. Like a hungry beast, it actually grew bigger and stronger as it devoured everything in its path.

It roared out of Biehle and continued east, feasting on forests and farms and killing another eight people.

FRANTIC FOR HELP

Meanwhile, the people of Annapolis and Biehle were in desperate shape. Hundreds were injured, and many were fighting for their lives, with crushed bones and bleeding wounds. There was no way to call for help. Few people in small towns had telephones in their homes. And those who did couldn't make calls, because telephone wires were down.

What made the
Tri-State Tornado so
unique was that it
actually grew bigger
and stronger as it
devoured everything
in its path.

One man managed to drive his motorcar out of the rubble-strewn streets of Annapolis. He drove thirty miles north to find a working phone. Frantic, he called the newspaper in St. Louis, the nearest big city. Word of the disaster started to spread. But it would be hours until help arrived.

Meanwhile, the tornado continued on its path of destruction.

Within the hour, more than six hundred people would be dead.

AN ENORMOUS BLACK CLOUD

Back in Parrish, nobody had any idea what was coming.

Adrian's father, John, had headed into town to pick up some farm supplies. His mother, Edna, was tending to the house and playing with little Wendell and Faye. At Parrish School, Adrian kept his eyes glued to the big classroom clock. School let out at 3:15 P.M., but he and four other boys were being dismissed early for the marbles tournament. It was being held outside the railroad depot, just a few minutes' walk from the school.

Roughly sixty miles to the west, the tornado was crossing the Mississippi River, which separates the state of Missouri from Illinois. The twister was now about three-quarters of a mile wide. And it no longer looked like a tornado. It was a roiling black cloud, so enormous that it seemed to stretch out across the entire sky. Its swirling winds were filled with tons of wreckage. There were shards of glass and slabs of wood and chunks of houses. Splintered tree limbs and dirt and mud were scoured up from the ground. There were thousands of objects stolen from homes, like pots and beds and quilts and books and toys. All of this was spinning around the body of the tornado at 300 miles per hour.

The tornado moved across the river, slurping up water as it crossed. The brown waters of the powerful Mississippi churned and foamed under the swirling winds.

Within minutes of crossing the river into Illinois, the tornado smashed into the small town of Gorham. In one minute—less time than it would take to make a bed—every single building in the town was destroyed. Twenty-seven people were killed.

Six minutes later it hit Murphysboro, a thriving city of twelve thousand people.

It had taken one hundred years for Murphysboro to grow from a scrappy railroad town into one of the most prosperous cities in Southern Illinois. It took less than two minutes for the heart of the city to be destroyed. The tornado smashed brick

It no longer looked like a tornado. It was a roiling black cloud, so enormous that it seemed to stretch out across the entire sky.

factories and mills, knocking them down as if they were sand castles. Cars and rooftops flew into the sky, never to be seen again. Railroad cars flew off tracks and landed hundreds of yards away.

In Murphysboro, 237 people lost their lives, more than any other community in the tornado's path.

But the tornado wasn't nearly finished.

Within minutes, it had struck its next victims, the small farming towns of De Soto and Bush. Both were almost totally demolished. At 2:38 P.M., the tornado plowed through West Frankfort, a large city just twelve miles southwest of Parrish. There, 127 people died.

The tornado had been on the ground for one hundred minutes. Behind it was a path of death and ruin more than one hundred miles long.

And now it had taken aim at Parrish.

In Murphysboro, two girls sit amid the wreckage of their home.

Only a few desks can
be seen in the wreckage
of one of Murphysboro's
elementary schools.

An elderly woman makes
her way through the
ruins of Murphysboro.

Rescuers were slow to reach
ruined towns. It was up
to local people to band
together to search through
the wreckage for survivors.

The ruins of the town of West Frankfort, Illinois, in the wake of the Tri-State Tornado, March 1925.

Little survived the tornado's fury. But some people managed to find some treasures in the ruins.

NOTHING LEFT

As the tornado was destroying West Frankfort, Adrian was finally heading to the marbles tournament. Four other boys would also be competing. It took only a few minutes for the five of them to walk from the school to the railroad depot.

It was just past 3:00 p.m., and the skies were growing purplish black, like an enormous bruise. Angry clouds boiled. Thunder growled in the distance. The boys groaned. Would the marbles tournament be canceled?

And then Adrian saw it: a rolling black cloud approaching quickly from the west. His blood turned to ice as he realized he was looking at a massive tornado.

At first the boys thought to take shelter in a small store.

But Adrian shook his head.

"We have to get back to school!" he shouted.

In a blink, the boys were sprinting across the railroad tracks and back toward the school. Rain started to fall. The day turned to night. They made it inside just as the tornado hit.

Crash!

All at once, every one of the school's windows shattered.

The building shuddered. Dirt and shards of wood flew through the air. A horrifying sound filled the air, a furious, crashing roar. The seconds dragged by. It seemed that any moment the school would be lifted into the sky.

At last the tornado passed. Adrian and the other terrified children crawled out of their hiding places. On shaking legs, Adrian, Ruie, Leonard, and the other students made their way out of the school. As he stepped outside, Adrian stared in shock.

All he could see, in any direction, was wreckage. Not a single building stood except the school and a church. Trees had been torn from the earth. Those left standing had been stripped of their branches. The scene looked more like a bombed-out battle-field than a peaceful small town.

Clutching one another's hands, the Dillon children headed out of the ruined town toward their farm. Their familiar landmarks were gone. The dirt path leading home was filled with debris—wagon wheels, smashed furniture, torn fabric, chunks of houses. Frightened cows and pigs huddled together. The children passed the spot where Adrian and his friends had stood before the tornado hit. The store where they almost took shelter was completely gone.

But even that could not prepare the Dillon kids for what they would find when they got home: Nothing. The house was gone. So was the barn.

They called for their parents, for Wendell and Faye. But their voices disappeared into the eerie silence. Adian fought back tears as one terrible thought rasped through his mind:

Everyone must be dead.

LOST AND FOUND

The scene was the same all across southern Missouri and Illinois. Stunned survivors searched desperately for their loved ones, clawing through rubble to reach those who were trapped. And still the tornado roared on. It crossed into Indiana, hitting the towns of Griffin, Owensville, and Princeton and killing four more people.

And then, finally, the tornado began to slow and shrink. At about 4:30 P.M., the monster tornado faded to a ghostly swirl. It took its last deadly breaths over a field in southern Indiana before finally disappearing.

At last, the Tri-State Tornado was dead.

Never before had a single tornado stayed on the ground for so long—three and a half hours. Never before had one tornado killed so many and

destroyed so much. By morning, the Tri-State Tornado was news all over the world.

For the rest of his long life, Adrian Dillon would try not to think about those terrible moments when he and Leonard and Ruie stood alone on their ruined farm. He would try to forget the sight of his shattered town.

But he would always cherish the memory of what came next: of seeing his mother walking toward them, clutching the hands of Faye and Wendell. The three had been carried away with their house, but dropped into a field without a scratch.

Not long after, a voice rang out: his father's. He had been inside a store when the tornado hit. He, too, had been lifted into the sky and then tumbled into a field. His leg was injured, but he managed to run back to the farm to find his family.

They huddled together in amazement and relief. The Tri-State Tornado had taken away everything they owned—their house, their barn, all of their possessions. Adrian had lost his prized marbles collection.

But the Dillons still had what was most precious, and all that mattered: one another.

THE TRI-STATE FILES

FIRST PICTURES OF STORM DISASTER

HERALD EXAMINER

1,000 DEAD, 3,000 HURT LATEST TOLL OF TORNADO

In the Twinkling of an Eye, Murphysboro Was No More

To this day, the Tri-State Tornado remains the deadliest single tornado ever to strike the United States. The disaster shocked the world, and helped change ideas about the dangers of tornadoes. Turn the page to learn more about this disaster.

MY RESEARCH JOURNEY

THE SPARK

Over the years, many I Survived readers have suggested that I write about the Tri-State Tornado. (They send me so many great ideas!)

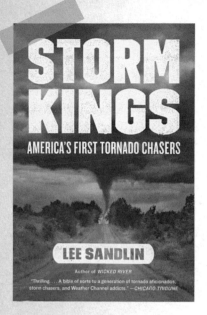

STORM KINGS

AMERICA'S FIRST TORNADO CHASERS

LEE SANDLIN

Author of *WICKED RIVER*

"Thrilling. . . . A bible of sorts to a generation of tornado aficionados, storm chasers, and Weather Channel addicts." —*CHICAGO TRIBUNE*

LEARNING MORE

These letters inspired me to learn more about historic tornadoes.

I read an incredible book called *Storm Kings* that took me back into early tornado science. I was fascinated!

FINDING ADRIAN

There are three great books about the Tri-State Tornado, and I read all of them. My colleague Allison Friedman discovered the book *Death Rides the Sky* by Angela Mason. This is where I read about Adrian Dillon.

I learned more details about the Dillons and life in Parrish by reading historical articles.

Tri-State Tornado of March 18, 1925

Death Rides The Sky

Incredible Survivor Stories of America's Worst Tornado

ANGELA MASON

THE TRI-STATE TORNADO
BY THE NUMBERS

235 miles
Length of tornado's path of destruction

Three hours and thirty minutes
Time on the ground

300 miles per hour
Estimated speed of winds

695
Number of people killed

2,027
Number of people injured

72 miles per hour
Maximum speed of tornado

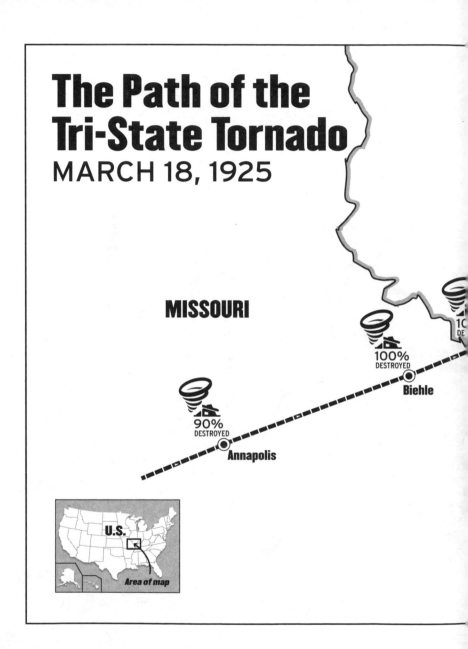

The Path of the Tri-State Tornado
MARCH 18, 1925

MISSOURI

100%
DESTROYED
Biehle

90%
DESTROYED
Annapolis

U.S.

Area of map

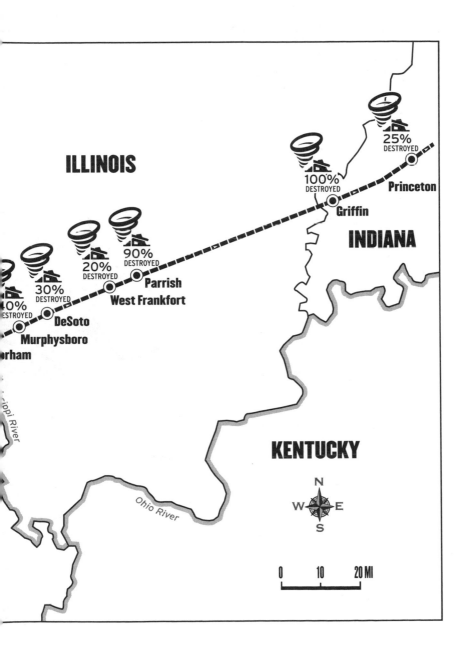

ILLINOIS

100%
DESTROYED

Griffin

25%
DESTROYED

Princeton

INDIANA

90%
DESTROYED

20%
DESTROYED

Parrish

30%
DESTROYED

West Frankfort

0%
ESTROYED

DeSoto

Murphysboro

rham

ippi River

Ohio River

KENTUCKY

N
W   E
S

0   10   20 MI

AFTER THE TORNADO

Shattered Lives, Shattered Land

A girl in her ruined
neighborhood in
De Soto, Illinois.
For months, many
survivors lived in
tents provided by the
United States Army.

Today, when disaster strikes, ambulances race down highways. Helicopters pluck people out of danger and fly them to hospitals. Huge trucks and airplanes can deliver supplies.

But in 1925, there were few highways. There were no helicopters, and airplanes were just beginning to zip across the skies. It took a very long time for rescuers to reach some of the towns destroyed by the Tri-State Tornado. And most of the aid arrived by train.

Rescue trains carried doctors, nurses, and supplies to wrecked towns, and brought the injured to hospitals in distant cities.

The Red Cross handed out tents and basic supplies.

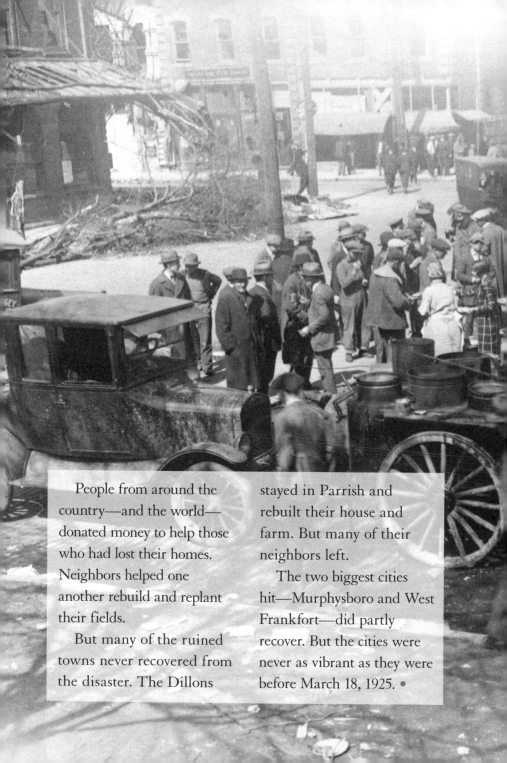

People from around the country—and the world—donated money to help those who had lost their homes. Neighbors helped one another rebuild and replant their fields.

But many of the ruined towns never recovered from the disaster. The Dillons stayed in Parrish and rebuilt their house and farm. But many of their neighbors left.

The two biggest cities hit—Murphysboro and West Frankfort—did partly recover. But the cities were never as vibrant as they were before March 18, 1925. •

In the days and weeks after the tornado, thousands of homeless people relied on free food provided by the Red Cross and other relief organizations.

IF YOU LIVED IN THE
1920s

The 1920s were nicknamed the "roaring twenties" because there was a sense of excitement and hope in the air. Life in America was changing—quickly. Here's what your life would have been like:

Just for Fun . . . Yum! Pie-eating contests were wildly popular across the country.

Roller skates were just invented!

TOP DOG German shepherds, with collies and terriers right behind.

You'd be eating . . .

Americans fell madly in love with chocolate in the 1920s. Some chocolate treats invented back then are still popular today.

You'd be talking about an amazing dog named Balto

A big news story in 1925 was about a Siberian husky Balto, and his musher, Gunnar Kaasen (below). They led a team of sled dogs on an emergency mission to deliver medicine to the city of Nome, Alaska.

In January, a deadly disease called diphteria was threatening Nome's children.

There was a medicine for diphtheria. But there was no way to get it to Nome; in winter, the city couldn't be reached by airplane or ship because of blizzards and ice.

The only hope was for teams of sled dogs to carry the medicine through six hundred miles of dangerous wildnerness.

Three different sled dog teams shared the journey.

But it was Balto and Kaasen who delivered the medicine to Nome.

They saved hundreds of lives—and became famous around the world.

OUR GANG
This was a film
series that
followed a group
of neighborhood
kids on their
adventures. When
they first began,
in 1922, they were
silent films.

Mom, is that you?

Women were just beginning to gain new rights in the 1920s. They won the right to vote in 1920. At the same time, many women rejected old-fashioned clothing.

They chopped off their long hair and traded ankle-skimming dresses for shorter styles.

69

ADVENTURES IN

In the 1890s, George Rodek used a hot-air balloon to rise into the sky and get a closer look at clouds and to take weather readings.

WEATHER SCIENCE

Before the days of weather satellites and radar, it wasn't easy to find out what was happening in the skies above.

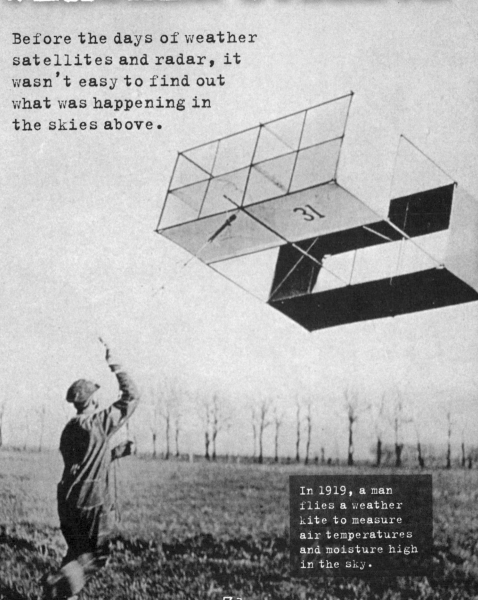

In 1919, a man flies a weather kite to measure air temperatures and moisture high in the sky.

John Finley:
Tornado Genius

John Park Finley was the first person to closely study tornadoes. At the time, most people believed tornadoes were rare. But Finley understood that they were all too common in some parts of America, and a big threat to the people living there.

He urged all people in tornado-prone areas to build "tornado caves," underground shelters to protect from tornado winds.

He also argued that weather forecasters should send out tornado warnings when violent thunderstorms were likely.

At the time, many people believed Finley was exaggerating the dangers of tornadoes. His work was ignored, and then mostly forgotten.

But guess what? He was right all along.

John Finley
was one of
the first
U.S. weather
forecasters.

History's
DEADLIEST
Tornadoes

1 The Tri-State Tornado, 1925

STATES: Missouri, Illinois, and Indiana
INTENSITY: EF5 **DEATHS:** 695 **INJURED:** 2,027

Wreckage of
the St. Louis
Tornado, 1896

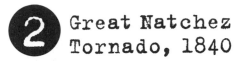

2 Great Natchez Tornado, 1840

STATE: Natchez, Mississippi
INTENSITY: Estimated EF5 **DEATHS:** 317+ **INJURED:** 109

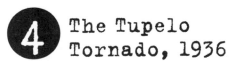

3 The St. Louis Tornado, 1896

STATE: St. Louis, Missouri
INTENSITY: EF4 **DEATHS:** 225+ **INJURED:** 1,000

4 The Tupelo Tornado, 1936

STATE: Tupelo, Mississippi
INTENSITY: EF5
DEATHS: 216+ **INJURED:** 700

5 The Gainesville Tornado, 1936

STATE: Gainesville, Georgia
INTENSITY: EF4
DEATHS: 203 **INJURED:** 1,600

#2

THE EVIL SWIRLING DARKNESS

THE TRUE STORY OF THE JOPLIN TORNADO, MAY 22, 2011

It was Sunday, May 22, 2011. Before the day was over, much of the city of Joplin, Missouri, would be in ruins. One hundred sixty-one people would be dead and more than one thousand injured.

But earlier that Sunday, what Ethan and Bennett Satterlee were thinking about was a birthday party. It was Bennett's eleventh birthday, and both boys were excited for an afternoon pool party at their grandparents' house. That morning after church, their mom, Shannon, had baked Bennett's favorite vanilla cake. Bennett and seven-year-old Ethan had taken heaping spoonfuls of

Joplin is tucked into the southwest corner of Missouri, where Kansas, Arkansas, and Missouri meet. (Below) A charming street in downtown Joplin.

leftover vanilla icing into the yard. They had devoured the delicious frosting with strawberries plucked from the family's garden.

It was a quiet morning in Joplin, a peaceful city of fifty thousand tucked into a corner of south-western Missouri. The city had sprung up 150 years before, and back then was mainly known for its dangerous coal mines and wild street fights.

But Joplin's rough days were long gone. Over the decades, Joplin had grown into a proud city of pretty parks, good schools, and quiet neighborhoods. The Satterlee boys felt lucky to be growing up here, not far from the house where their dad had lived as a kid.

Laughing and relaxing in their yard on that Sunday morning, the last thing Bennett and Ethan could imagine was that their city was about to be struck by one of the deadliest tornadoes in US history.

JOPLIN'S GRITTY PAST

Right: One hundred years ago, Joplin's skies were blackened by coal smoke.

Below right: Most men worked in the area's mines, where they spent long days underground inhaling toxic fumes.

Below: The city became famous in 1933 when two legendary bank robbers known as Bonnie and Clyde hid out in Joplin while running from police.

VIEW IN THE "ATTIE" MINE

CHASING VIOLENT STORMS

As the Satterlees planned for Bennett's party, a storm chaser named Jeff Piotrowski was 230 miles away from Joplin, at his home in Norman, Oklahoma. For more than thirty-five years, Jeff had been studying supercell thunderstorms. These are the violent storms that sometimes unleash tornadoes.

Jeff was looking over the weather forecast for that day. And what he saw worried him. The last month, April 2011, had been one of the most violent weather months in history. An incredible 758 tornadoes had touched down in the United States in April. One of those twisters had killed sixty-four people in the college town of Tuscaloosa, Alabama.

May had been quieter. But now the skies were angry again.

For days, Jeff had been keeping his eye on a large and dangerous storm system. It had formed over the waters off Alaska, four thousand miles away. It had crept down the West Coast to California, and then swept across the Rocky Mountains. As it traveled east, it gained strength.

Over the past few days, the storm had dumped two feet of snow on Denver, Colorado. It had blasted Texas with hailstones as big as apples. Over Kansas it became deadly, firing off a small tornado that killed a fifty-three-year-old man.

Jeff and other weather experts believed that this storm system would grow even stronger. They worried that it could join forces with another storm system that was moving up from the south. Conditions were shaping up for dangerous tornadoes later that Sunday afternoon.

But exactly when would they strike? And where?

THE MOTHER
OF TORNADOES

Supercell thunderstorms
are bigger, more powerful,
and more dangerous than
regular thunderstorms.
On a radar screen, they
look like mini hurricanes,
with swirling winds. They
often produce flooding
rains, hailstones, and,
sometimes, tornadoes.

INVISIBLE MONSTERS

Today, weather scientists (known as meteorologists) can predict many kinds of weather with amazing accuracy.

Weather satellites floating above Earth have cameras that can spot hurricanes the moment they start to swirl. Powerful radar can measure rainfall and wind speeds inside a raging thunderstorm. A skilled meteorologist can tell you a week in advance whether your Little League game could be rained out or if you'll need snow boots for recess.

Tornadoes, however, remain stubbornly mysterious.

Scientists know that tornadoes form inside supercell thunderstorms. But only 20 percent of supercells cause tornadoes. And it's impossible to know for sure which supercells will launch killer twisters and which will fizzle out.

And even after a tornado has formed inside a supercell, it's still impossible to see. The most

April 2011 had been one of the most violent weather months in US history. That month, an incredible 758 tornadoes had touched down in the United States.

powerful radar cannot get a clear picture of what is happening inside the swirling clouds of a thunderstorm. Tornadoes are like secretive monsters coming to life inside dark caves. They remain completely hidden until they roar out of the storm clouds to devour everything in their paths. As of now, there is only one tool that can detect that a tornado is on the way: the human eye. Somebody must actually see one as it bursts out of the sky.

EYES IN THE SKY

Weather satellites
in space beam down
photographs that enable
forecasters to track
weather systems and
storms as they move
across Earth.

Storm chasers Jeff and Kathryn Piotrowski

TORNADOES UP CLOSE

Most weather forecasters predicted storms along the border of Kansas and Missouri—near Joplin. By 11:00 a.m., Jeff Piotrowski and his wife, Kathryn, were in their Chevy Avalanche truck, hoping to catch up with the storm by late afternoon. Jeff was at the wheel, and Kathryn sat next to him with a video camera charged and ready. This was their weekend routine during tornado season. They sometimes drove one thousand miles or more on their weekend chases. And they were not alone. There are often hundreds of storm chasers on the roads during tornado season.

For some people, storm chasing is a thrilling hobby, a chance to see one of nature's most powerful forces up close. They speed after violent weather, hoping to come home with awesome videos to post on YouTube.

But others, like the Piotrowskis, are working to unravel the secrets of tornadoes. These men and women often work as "storm spotters" for the National Weather Service. They provide early warnings that tornadoes are coming, which helps save lives. Over the years, tornado videos captured by storm chasers have helped scientists better understand storms and tornadoes.

Of course, chasing after a supercell thunderstorm is extremely dangerous. Tornadoes can appear suddenly. They can change directions without warning. Winds traveling 200 miles per hour can peel a storm chaser's car off a highway

STUDYING NATURE'S FURY

Tornado researchers often risk their lives to gather information about tornadoes and other extreme storms. Here, a group of scientists monitor a supercell in Nebraska.

and send it spinning through the air. Small stones become bullets that shatter windshields.

Over the years, Jeff Piotrowski has witnessed more than 850 tornado strikes. Few people appreciate the terrifying power of tornadoes better than he does. Still, nothing prepared Jeff for what he would later witness in Joplin, Missouri.

FALSE ALARMS

Like most people in Joplin, the Satterlees heard that severe thunderstorms were predicted for later that day. That was disappointing; they'd have to move Bennett's afternoon party from poolside back to their house. Weather forecasts warned of a tornado risk, but few in Joplin paid much attention.

True, Joplin had been struck twice by deadly tornadoes in the 1970s. In 1971, a twister badly damaged parts of the city and killed a college student. Just two years later, another tornado

Joplin residents clean up after a tornado that struck the city in 1973.

Good Morning
Today Is
Saturday, May 12, 1973
VOL. LXXVII, NO. 276

The Joplin Globe

JOPLIN, MISSOURI—TWENTY-EIGHT PAGES

Mild
Partly cloudy; high today in upper 60s or low 70s; low tonight 44-50

PRICE Daily 15c Sunday 25c

More Than 100 Injured . . .

Tornadic Windstorm Kills 3 Persons, Causes Estimated $20 Million Damage

The Joplin area is still reeling from the onlaught of massive gale force winds which struck the entire city early Friday morning, causing millions of dollars in property damage, claiming the lives of three persons and injuring more than 100 others.

The storm struck the city shortly before 7 a.m., with winds estimated to have reached speeds of 70 to 100 miles per hour, accompanied by hail. In a matter of minutes, the ground was covered with about two inches of marble - sized hail.

Some of those who inspected the

have a hurricane here, but it was like a hurricane."

No section of the city escaped at least partial damage during the brief storm. Numerous manufacturing plants, businesses, mobile homes and other buildings were destroyed or heavily damaged.

City officials estimate the damage at well in excess of $20 million, which would make this the worst storm ever to strike Joplin. Public works officials feel that more than 1,000 trees in the city were blown over by the storm.

West Side Trailer Court, located on West 7th Street about three miles west of Joplin.

Mrs. Loyd Gilpin, who with her husband owns the trailer court, says 23 mobile homes were in the park and that 11 were destroyed. Numerous small children were in the trailers when the storm struck without warning.

(A list of persons requiring hospital treatment after the storm appears on Page 4A.)

Miller Manufacturing Co., Inc., located in southeast Joplin at 27th Street and Davis Boulevard.

Employes estimated that about 200 persons had reported for work at the industry, which manufactures industrial clothing, when the storm hit.

"We were mostly in the offices and cafeteria when it came," one employe said struck in the middle of the night, killing three. A ten-year-old girl woke up as she was flying through the sky on her mattress. Amazingly, she landed safely, terrified but uninjured.

These two tornadoes put the city on alert. The city installed tornado sirens mounted on poles. The sirens sounded during severe storms, when tornadoes were possible.

But years went by with no tornadoes. By 2011, it had been almost forty years since the city had been struck. Meanwhile, there had been hundreds of warnings over the years, and the sound of the sirens was familiar during the spring. There had been so many false alarms that few people even took the sirens seriously anymore. To many, the sirens were more irritating than frightening, like the whining of an annoying little kid.

Early in the afternoon, while the skies were still clear, Bennett and Ethan had gone to their grand-parents' for a quick pre-party swim. The weather forecast was getting worse, but Joplin bustled as usual. Stores like Home Depot and Walmart were crowded with shoppers running their weekend errands. Playgrounds rang with shrieks and laughs. Joplin High School's eight hundred seniors were at their graduation ceremony, grinning for the cameras of their proud parents.

By 4:30 p.m., the sky was filled with dark clouds, and rain had started to fall. By then, Bennett had returned home and some party guests had started to arrive. Ethan was with his uncle Frank, aunt Sana, and cousin Wyatt. They were set to arrive at the party any minute.

At 5:11 p.m., Joplin's twenty-eight tornado sirens blared.

Weeeaaaah!
Weeeaaaah!

Looking out a window, the Satterlees saw nothing but pouring rain. Another false alarm, it seemed. Still, Bennett's mom sent the kids to the basement and turned on the TV to monitor weather reports. She called Uncle Frank on his cell phone. "We're getting close," he promised.

GIGANTIC GRAY CLOUD

Jeff and Kathryn Piotrowski arrived in Joplin just a few minutes later. They rode slowly through the city's downtown. Kathryn admired the historic buildings. Some had been built back in the late 1800s, when Joplin was a wild town known for its coal mines and street fights.

The city seemed calm.

But then Jeff saw it: a boiling gray cloud moving in from the west. He slowed the car and stared at the cloud more intently. His blood turned to ice as he realized that it wasn't really a cloud.

It was an enormous tornado.

Two violent supercells had joined together to create a storm of unimaginable power.

What made this tornado especially dangerous was that it had become "rain-wrapped." It had formed in a cornfield outside Joplin and then became wrapped up in a curtain of rain.

When people think of tornadoes, most picture a perfect funnel. But rain-wrapped tornadoes, which look just like big storm clouds, are common. In fact, the huge tornado that destroyed Tuscaloosa, Alabama, the month before had been rain-wrapped. Many there didn't realize it was a tornado until it was too late to take shelter.

THE JOPLIN
TORNADO IS BORN

This grainy image
comes from a video
taken by a group of
storm chasers called
Basehunters Chasing.
It shows the Joplin
Tornado moments after
it formed, over a
field to the west
of the city.

Jeff Piotrowski making his frantic call to a 911
operator during the Joplin tornado.

Many in Joplin spotted the giant gray cloud moving across the sky. Few understood what they were seeing. Jeff Piotrowski quickly called 911, shouting into his cell phone that there was a massive tornado heading right into southern Joplin. On the side of the road, a policeman sat in his cruiser. Jeff stopped the truck and leaped out.

"That's a dangerous tornado!" he cried, pointing up at the approaching gray cloud. "Get the sirens going! Get the sirens going!"

By then, weather forecasters throughout the region realized that Joplin was in grave danger. Jeff had been right all along. Two violent supercells had crashed together to create a storm of unimaginable power. And now it was about to devour the city of Joplin.

Thanks to Jeff Piotrowski's warning to the policeman, Joplin's sirens sounded again at 5:31 p.m. It was extremely unusual for the city's sirens to sound twice in such a short period of time. Most people understood: This was no false alarm.

VICIOUS ATTACK

Throughout Joplin, people rushed for shelter. The lucky ones headed for storm cellars dug into their backyards. These small underground rooms are the only truly safe places in a strong tornado. Others ran to their basements or huddled in closets. They pulled pillows from beds and climbed into bathtubs.

Along Joplin's busy shopping streets, people left their cars and hustled into stores like Walmart and Home Depot. At fast-food restaurants, managers herded customers into walk-in refrigerators with strong metal walls. The Satterlees and their guests packed into a small storage room in their basement. This small concrete-walled space doubled as the family's tornado shelter.

Outside, the tornado, still gaining strength, began its vicious attack on the city.

It was no longer just a cloud of swirling air. And it was filled with pieces of Joplin that it had sucked up from the ground. There were chunks of houses and parts of cars, tree branches and furniture, shards of glass and clumps of dirt.

```
It seemed like hours
   before the noise
 stopped, until the
  tornado finally
finished with the house.
```

The monstrous twister was now a staggering three-quarters of a mile wide. Its 200-mile-per-hour winds pulverized brick buildings, turned houses into piles of splintered wood and shattered glass, and hurled cars and trucks thousands of feet into the air.

It ripped the roof off Home Depot, demolished a Chick-fil-A and Burger King, and turned a Walgreens drugstore into a pile of rubble. It wrecked six schools, including Joplin High School.

From the basement of the Sattlerlees' house, the family and their guests could hear deafening crashes and thuds above them. It was the sound of their home being ripped apart, of years' worth of treasures being crushed and swept away.

It seemed like hours before the noise finally stopped, until the tornado finally finished with their house and moved on.

Slowly, the family and their friends emerged from the storage room. They walked up the stairs to discover their house was in ruins. Rain was pouring through missing chunks of roof. Walls had collapsed. Furniture was smashed.

But it wasn't the house they were thinking about. It was Ethan, Wyatt, Frank, and Sara. Peering into their wrecked neighborhood, there was no sign of Ethan and the others. They were still somewhere outside, in the evil swirling darkness.

TORN TO PIECES

Around the same time, the Piotrowskis were still driving in their truck, trying to steer clear of the tornado. It was terrifyingly close, and moving at highway speed: 60 miles per hour. The road had become an obstacle course of fallen telephone poles, sizzling wires, and pieces of rooftops and other debris. Deadly chunks of wreckage flew through the air like bombs being dropped from the sky.

Jeff struggled to keep the tornado in sight as he drove. It was to the left of them, moving in the opposite direction from the truck. But at any moment it could change direction and swerve into their path. Both Jeff and Kathryn fought panic. They knew they were in grave danger. If the tornado made a sudden turn, they could be sucked into its jaws, or crushed by debris.

But, luckily, the tornado stayed on its path, and soon the Piotrowskis had driven clear of its winds. They were out of danger.

But their relief soon turned to horror as they drove into a neighborhood that had suffered a direct hit. What had once been a road of tidy houses was now a sea of wreckage. Houses had been shredded, cars smashed. Never in Jeff's decades of storm chasing had he seen such utter destruction. All across the city, the scene was the same.

The tornado caused
fires to erupt
throughout the city.

In seconds, entire neighborhoods were completely destroyed.

St. John's hospital took a direct hit by the tornado and had to be evacuated.

The tornado
destroyed
six schools
in Joplin.

Many people
lost almost
everything
they owned.

Giant stores, including this Home Depot, became death traps in the tornado.

Tornadoes are rated by their size and strength on a scale known as the Enhanced Fujita Scale. An EF1 tornado is a small twister that knocks over garbage cans and small trees. The Joplin tornado was an EF5—the strongest kind. These monstrous twisters can destroy most buildings, yank trains off their tracks, and pick up tractor-trailer trucks as if they were toys.

FAITH AND NEIGHBORS

Many people were trapped in the wreckage of homes and stores. Hundreds were horribly injured. Many staggered through the doors of St. John's hospital, which was closest to the damage zone. But the hospital building had taken a direct hit. Nurses had thrown themselves on top of patients to protect them from flying glass and debris. Rooms were demolished. Six people were dead. There was no power, and water gushed from broken pipes. Doctors and nurses worked

ENHANCED FUJITA SCALE FOR TORNADOES

Wind Speed	EF Scale	Typical Damage
65–85 mph	0	Minor or no damage
86–110 mph	1	Moderate damage
111–135 mph	2	Considerable damage
136–165 mph	3	Severe damage
166–200 mph	4	Extreme damage
200+ mph	5	Total destruction of buildings

ONLY 2 PERCENT OF TORNADOES ARE EF5

heroically to save lives. One doctor did surgery in an operating room lit only by a flashlight. Nurses comforted the injured. But many feared that the building could collapse. The building had to be evacuated.

Fortunately, Joplin's other major hospital, Freeman, was only one mile away. And it had come through the tornado untouched. A small army of volunteers with pickup trucks transported the wounded and nurses from St. John's to Freeman. School buses arrived to drive others.

At Freeman, doctors and nurses quickly mobilized. On a typical night, there are four doctors working in Freeman's emergency room. Within hours, 135 doctors were at the hospital. They stopped patients' bleeding, stitched up wounds, and set broken bones.

Emergency workers from neighboring cities and towns rushed to Joplin and helped pull people from rubble and care for the injured.

All across the city, ordinary people turned themselves into emergency workers. Neighbors helped neighbors, tearing through piles of wreckage with their bare hands to reach those who were trapped. The Satterlees prayed that Ethan, Wyatt, Frank, and Sana were unhurt. But they were soon out in their neighborhood, helping free people who were trapped. The Piotrowskis helped, too.

"I knew we had witnessed one of the deadliest tornadoes in modern times," Jeff says.

And it was. The Joplin Tornado, America's deadliest in sixty years, killed 161 people.

THE GREATEST GIFT

For the Satterlees, though, the day did not end in tragedy.

Uncle Frank's truck finally appeared. The back window was shattered. The metal was dented and battered. But Frank, Sana, Ethan, and Wyatt were all safe.

Ethan knows that he will likely never forget the terrifying moments when the tornado gripped the truck, when the window was smashed and glass sprayed over him, when he feared he might never see his family again.

But sharing their stories from that day, the Satterlee boys do not dwell on their frightening memories or all that the family lost. They speak of the power of their faith, the strength of their community, and the generosity of the thousands of people from around the country who came to help heal their wounded city.

Looking back on his eleventh birthday, Bennett knows he received the greatest gift imaginable. "My family survived the tornado."

Left: Ethan and Bennett's parents, Shannon and Barrett, watch as their ruined house is demolished.

The Sattlerlees outside their rebuilt home, from left: Bennett, Shannon, Barrett, Carolyn, and Ethan.

THE JOPLIN FILES

Joplin is a small city that sits near where three states meet: Missouri, Arkansas, and Kansas. I wrote about Joplin in *I Survived the Joplin Tornado, 2011*, but for me the city is far more than just a book topic. The city continues to inspire me with its resilience, and I am lucky to be in touch  with many people that I met through my research process.

Turn the page to learn more.

MY JOURNEY TO JOPLIN, MISSOURI

How this small Missouri city captured my imagination—and my heart.

AN INVITATION

I received many emails from kids and parents from Joplin suggesting that I write an I Survived book about their city.

A FIRST VISIT

I visited Joplin for the first time in 2014 to research the story, and then wrote *I Survived the Joplin Tornado, 2011.* After that visit, I received a note from Mrs. Satterlee telling me that Ethan wanted to share his story.

A RETURN TO JOPLIN

In September 2015, I was able to return to Joplin to meet librarians, teachers, and hundreds of kids. I visited eleven schools and even got to have dinner with the Satterlees at their beautiful home. The visit was unforgettable.

(Above) A highlight of my trip to Joplin was finally meeting the Satterlee clan in person. Shannon makes the best chicken and rice soup ever.

(Below) Dr. Katherine Cornelius was on duty at Freeman Hospital the night of the tornado. Here she is with her kids, Jack and Sydney.

(Above) The amazing librarians of Joplin. From left: Sara Hart, Linda Sharp, Stephanie Prather, Lauren, Ashley Tucker, Katie Moore, Vanessa Gage, and Suzy Elliott.

THE STRENGTH OF JOPLIN

In the first months after the tornado struck Joplin, many worried that the city would never recover. The twister had destroyed so much—more than 7,000 houses, hundreds of businesses, churches, and schools. Could Joplin actually rebuild? Would it ever be the thriving city it once was?

The answer is yes.

First Visit

I first visited Joplin in December 2014, about three and a half years after the tornado. I went after receiving many emails from people from Joplin suggesting that I write about their city in the I Survived series.

I was fortunate to connect with a group of Joplin's elementary school librarians who agreed to be my guides to Joplin.

Tornado Scars

One of these fine women, Ashley Tucker, helped organize my trip, and then drove me through the heart of the disaster zone. I could see few scars of the tornado's damage. Most areas had been almost completely rebuilt.

I visited some of Joplin's new elementary schools. They are among the most modern and beautiful I'd ever seen. Joplin students chose the colors on the walls. Perhaps most important: Each classroom has a tornado safe room. And each school doubles as a tornado shelter for the neighborhood.

A Gift

Within five years of the tornado, there were actually more people in Joplin than before the disaster. The Satterlees' home was rebuilt, and the boys still feel lucky to live in Joplin.

Of course, those who lost family and friends still

grieve. The tragedy left scars, including many that cannot be easily seen.

Like many outsiders, I am amazed by the strength of so many people I met in Joplin. For me, perhaps nothing symbolizes that strength more than a

Above: Volunteers help a homeowner clean up and pick through wreckage. Rebuilding begins after the wreckage is finally cleared.

The beautiful library at Joplin's rebuilt Irving Elementary School.

A memorial in Joplin's Cunningham Park.

gift I received a few weeks after my second trip to Joplin, in October 2015.

It arrived in a large box. It was from the Satterlee family.

Inside the box was a large wooden cross. Shannon's note explained that it was made out of wreckage of the Joplin tornado.

The cross hangs over my desk at home. It reminds me that the story of Joplin is not only one of disaster and tragedy. It is one of hope, faith, and healing. •

THE JOPLIN TORNADO
BY THE NUMBERS

200

13 miles
Length of tornado's path of destruction

126,800
Number of volunteers who helped in the cleanup

6,954
Number of houses destroyed

miles per hour
Speed of Joplin Tornado's wind

3/4 of a mile
Width of tornado at widest point

15,000
Number of cars and trucks
picked up and destroyed

161
Number of
people
killed

$3 billion
Cost of rebuilding

WHY THE US IS THE
WORLD CAPITAL
OF TORNADOES

Violent storms happen when hot and cold air crashes together over the earth. Nowhere does this happen more often than in the middle of the United States. During the spring, cold air sweeps down from the Arctic over Canada, and then into the United States. At the same time, moist and hot air comes up from the Gulf of Mexico. Stormy weather often flies in from the west and gains power as it crosses the Rocky Mountains.

This is why the biggest and most violent tornadoes often happen in Oklahoma, Kansas, Nebraska, and northern Texas. This area is known as Tornado Alley.

FACT:
3/4 of all tornadoes on Earth happen in the US.

ARCTIC
OCEAN

Hudson
Bay

**Freezing air rushes
down from Canada**

CANADA

ROCKY MOUNTAINS

APPALACHIAN MOUNTAINS

Tornado Alley ➤

UNITED
STATES

ATLANTIC
OCEAN

**Warm, moist air rushes up
from Gulf of Mexico**

Gulf of
Mexico

PACIFIC
OCEAN

MEXICO

N
W · E
S

Caribbean
Sea

CAN YOU SPEAK TORNADO?

An Extreme Weather Glossary

Meteorologist A person who studies the science of weather.

Tornado Watch An official alert sent out to tell people that there are storms in the area that could cause tornadoes.

Tornado Warning A warning sent out by the weather service when an actual tornado funnel has been seen. (A tornado warning is more serious than a tornado watch.)

Funnel cloud A cone-shaped cloud with strong swirling winds. Once a funnel cloud hits the ground, it is officially called a tornado.

Cyclone Another word for tornado.

Waterspout A tornado over water.

Supercell A powerful thunderstorm capable of creating tornadoes.

Tornado Alley A name for the area of the United States from South Dakota to northern Texas, where most tornadoes happen each year.

Doppler A kind of radar used to track supercells and other storms.

The Man Called Mr. Tornado

Ted Fujita changed our understanding of tornadoes.

You've heard of the Fujita Scale, which is used to rate the strength of tornadoes. It's named for the scientist who invented it, Tetsuya "Ted" Fujita. From the 1950s until he died in 1998, Fujita dedicated his life to studying tornadoes.

When a large tornado struck, he would visit the area and inspect the damage. He collected photographs and films of tornadoes and studied them for months. He was one of the first to understand how tornadoes formed inside supercells. A version of the Fujita Scale is still used today (now it is known as the Enhanced Fujita Scale).

By the time he died in 1998, Fujita was respected around the world. Many called him by his nickname: Mr. Tornado.

Hail Horrors

Tornadoes aren't the only danger in a powerful storm.

These hailstones are about the size of baseballs. But they can be even larger.

A Missouri farmer and his son show off hailstones they collected in the spring of 1975.

Hail can shatter windshields, destroy crops, and cause serious injuries.

FACT:
About 25 people are badly injured by hail each year.

THE WORLD OF STORM CHASERS

Today's tornado hunters use high-tech gear

A TORNADO-PROOF CAR

This tricked-out chasing car has armored sides, bulletproof glass, and built-in radar and cameras. If caught in high winds, "tornado spikes" will anchor the car to the ground.

CHASER TRAFFIC JAM

During tornado season, dozens of chasers might be chasing the same storm. Many travel in vehicles topped by satellite dishes so that they can receive the most current weather information.

INSIDE A STORM-CHASING VAN

Chasers often travel in teams, in vans outfitted with computers and other high-tech storm-tracking tools.

WHEN A STORM CHASE TURNS DEADLY

The death of a famed tornado
hunter shows the risks of
chasing violent storms.

Tim Samaras
chasing a
storm in
2005.

Storm chasing is exciting and important work. But it is also dangerous. Without warning, a chaser can get caught in a storm's deadly grip. This is what happened to Tim Samaras, one of America's most famous and beloved storm chasers.

Tornado Fanatic

Samaras was a gifted engineer and a tornado fanatic. He built his own instruments to measure the strength of tornadoes and the sounds inside them. He had his own show, *Storm Chasers*, and was featured in many books and articles. He was beloved for his enthusiasm and respected for his caution.

On May 31, 2013, Samaras was chasing a tornado in El Reno, Oklahoma. He was with his twenty-four-year-old son Paul and his storm-chasing partner, Carl Young. Suddenly the tornado disappeared behind a curtain of rain and grew into a monster more than two miles wide. It caught Samaras's car and carried it more than a half mile before dropping it in a field. All three men lost their lives.

This was the first time storm chasers were killed on the job. But experts fear that the growing popularity of storm chasing means that more lives are at risk. •

Samaras, second from right, in 2005. His chasing partner, Carl Young, is to his left.

STAYING SAFE IN TORNADOES

You can't stop a tornado, but you can take steps to protect yourself.

1. Watch the Weather
This is especially important if you live in a tornado-prone area.

2. Take Warnings Seriously
If you are urged to take shelter, do so immediately. Don't wait until you can see a tornado.

3. Get Inside
It is not safe to be outdoors or in a car. If you don't have a tornado shelter, try to get to a basement.

4. Get Away from Windows
Stay away from corners, outside walls, and doors. If possible, get under a heavy table or desk.

5. Cover Your Head
Many storm chasers wear bike or ski helmets to protect themselves from flying debris.

6. Practice with Your Family
Make a family plan for where to shelter at home and how you will reconnect after the storm.

TORNADO SAFE ROOM
REFUGIO CONTRA TORNADOS

A sign at Joplin's rebuilt Irving Elementary School

In a powerful tornado, an underground shelter is the only truly safe place.

ACKNOWLEDGMENTS

To my Joplin friends: Suzy Elliott, Vanessa Gage, Katie Moore, Stephanie Prader, Linda Sharp, and Ashley Tucker, I feel so lucky to be connected to all of you. Special thanks to Ashley for organizing my trips to Joplin and guiding me through the city.

Ethan and Bennett Satterlee, thank you for sharing your experiences in the tornado, and Shannon and Barrett Satterlee, thank you for trusting me to tell your family's story.

I am grateful to Jeff and Kathryn Piotrowski for describing their Joplin chase for me, and to Kathryn for sharing her photos.

Thank you to Professor Edward Guinan from Villanova University who reviewed the manuscript and offered his expertise on tornado science.

To Deb Dinger, thank you for the endless work and dedication you poured into this book.

Our creative partnership over more than two decades is one of the joys of my life.

Nancy Mercado, I am enduringly grateful for your editorial wisdom, your friendship and your imperturbability as we bring these books to life.

Enormous thanks to the entire I Survived team, with extra hugs for Julie Amitie, Emily Heddleson, Gail Hochman, Beth Noble, Monica Palenzuela, Charisse Meloto, Robin Hoffman, and Jeffrey West.

To David, Leo, Jeremy, Dylan, Val, Mom, Dad, Steffi, Andrew, and my wonderful family, you are my shelter in every storm.

MY SOURCES

This book is the result of many hours of research and dozens of books, articles, interviews, websites, blogs, and videos. Below are my main sources.

America's Deadliest Twister: The Tri-State Tornado of 1925, by Geoff Partlow Carbondale, Illinois: Southern Illinois University Press, 2014

Storm Chasing the Joplin EF5 Tornado, DVD by Jeff and Kathryn Piotrowski

Death Rides the Sky: The Story of the 1925 Tri-State Tornado, by Angela Mason: Rockford, Illnois: Black Oak Media, 2011

The Forgotten Storm: The Great Tri-State Tornado of 1925, by Wallace Akin. Guilford, Conneticut: Lyons Press, 2002

Franklin County Illinois, 1818–1997. Paducah, Kentucky: Turner Publishing Company, 1996

"The Gathering Storm: Tracing the Trail of Joplin's Killer Tornado," by Cindy Hoedel and Lisa Gutierrez. *Kansas City Star*, December 11, 2011

Hunting Nature's Fury, by Roger Hill with Peter Bronski. Berkley, California: Wilderness Press, 2009

Storm Kings, by Lee Sandlin. New York: Pantheon Books, 2013

The Tri-State Tornado: The Story of America's Greatest Tornado Disaster, by Peter S. Felknor. Lincoln, Nebraska: iUniverse, 2004

Tornadoes: What They Are and How to Escape Them, by John P. Finley. Washington, DC: J. H. Soulé, 1888. Paperback 2008.

Tornado Hunter, by Stefan Bechtel with Tim Samaras. Washington, DC: National Geographic, 2009

Interviews with Shannon, Ethan, and Bennett Satterlee

Interviews with Jeff and Kathryn Piotrowski

157

PHOTO CREDITS

Maps by Jim McMahon

ABOUT THE AUTHOR

Photo by David Dreyfuss

Lauren Tarshis's *New York Times* bestselling I Survived series tells stories of young people and their resilience and strength in the midst of unimaginable disasters. Lauren has brought her signature warmth and exhaustive research to topics such as the September 11 attacks, the destruction of Pompeii, Hurricane Katrina, and the bombing of Pearl Harbor, among others. In addition to being the editor of Scholastic's *Storyworks* magazine and group editorial director for language arts for Scholastic classroom magazines, Lauren is also the author of the critically acclaimed novels *Emma-Jean Lazarus Fell Out of a Tree* and *Emma-Jean Lazarus Fell in Love*. She lives in Westport, Connecticut, and can be found online at www.laurentarshis.com.

ABOUT STORYWORKS

Storyworks is an award-winning classroom magazine read by more than 1 million kids in grades three to six. Combining thrilling stories and articles across genres plus amazing teacher support and online resources, *Storyworks* is a beloved and powerful language arts resource.

For more information go to:
www.scholastic.com/storyworks